I KNOW
RANCHERS

GRIDDLING

GRIDDLING

Fran Warde

hamlyn

Published in the UK in 1998
by Hamlyn, a division of Octopus Publishing Group Ltd
2–4 Heron Quays, London E14 4JP

This edition published 2002 by Octopus Publishing Group Ltd

Copyright ©1998, 2002 Octopus Publishing Group Ltd

ISBN 0 600 60821 2

Printed in China

NOTES

Both metric and imperial measurements have been given in all
recipes. Use one set of measurements only and not a
mixture of both.

Standard level spoon measurements are used in all recipes.
1 tablespoon = one 15 ml spoon
1 teaspoon = one 5 ml spoon

Eggs should be medium unless otherwise stated.
The Department of Health advises that eggs should not be
consumed raw. This book contains dishes made with raw or
lightly cooked eggs. It is prudent for more vulnerable people
such as pregnant and nursing mothers, invalids, the elderly,
babies and young children to avoid uncooked or lightly cooked
dishes made with eggs. Once prepared, these dishes should
be kept refrigerated and used promptly.

Meat and poultry should be cooked thoroughly. To test if poultry
is cooked, pierce the flesh through the thickest part with a
skewer or fork – the juices should run clear, never pink or red.

Milk should be full fat unless otherwise stated.

Do not re-freeze a dish that has been frozen previously.

Pepper should be freshly ground black pepper unless
otherwise stated.

Fresh herbs should be used unless otherwise stated. If
unavailable, use dried herbs as an alternative but halve the
quantities stated.

Measurements for canned food have been given as a standard
metric equivalent.

Nuts and nut derivatives
This book includes dishes made with nuts and nut derivatives.
It is advisable for customers with known allergic reactions to
nuts and nut derivatives and those who may be potentially
vulnerable to these allergies, such as pregnant and nursing
mothers, invalids, the elderly, babies and children, to avoid
dishes made with nuts and nut oils. It is also prudent to check
the labels of pre-prepared ingredients for the possible inclusion
of nut derivatives.

Ovens should be preheated to the specified temperature – if
using a fan-assisted oven, follow the manufacturer's
instructions for adjusting the time and the temperature.

Contents

Introduction

Now that good quality griddle pans are widely available, more and more people are discovering the pleasures and benefits of this versatile method of cooking. Cooking with a griddle pan is gratifyingly easy. It is also fun, fast and produces sensational results. *Griddling* has a mouth-watering range of imaginative recipes, created with a light, expert touch, and simply bursting with good flavours. The recipes use a repertoire of ingredients that are very much in keeping with today's food trends – fusing ingredients from East and West and using lots of herbs and flavourings with flair and confidence. Moreover, the sheer variety of dishes that can be cooked in a griddle pan is very appealing – the emphasis is on crisp, new vegetables, fresh fish, good quality poultry and game, and various kinds of meat. You will also enjoy cooking some of the delightful fruit recipes in your griddle pan.

LOW FAT BENEFITS

One of the main benefits of griddling is that you do not need to use oil or fat in the actual cooking process. This is certainly the case with the convenient non-stick griddle pans. Some people prefer to brush pans that do not have a non-stick surface with a little oil, but once you acquire the knack of using the pan correctly you can cook very

successfully without it. This is why griddling is a very attractive cooking method for those who prefer a low-fat cooking style. With this approach in mind, the recipes in this book have been created with the freshest, healthiest ingredients.

THE GRIDDLE PAN

As griddling has become increasingly popular, a wide range of pans has become available, so the choice is very wide. The griddle looks like a frying pan, but has distinctive ridges across the cooking surface. When you pick it up you will notice that it is significantly heavier than the normal frying pan – this is because it has to withstand very high temperatures. The pan may have a spout on the side for pouring off juices and it may be round or square in shape. The basic method is to pre-heat the griddle pan so that the surface is very hot before starting to cook. Then the food is quickly seared on both sides to form a crust that will seal in the juices and lock in the flavours. This crust must form before the food is turned over to sear on the other side, otherwise it will stick to the pan. As soon as it is seared on both sides, the heat is quickly lowered for the remaining cooking time, allowing the food to cook thoroughly inside without burning outside. Once you

have the knack, you will find this an effortless and really enjoyable way of preparing food.

LOOKING AFTER YOUR PAN

When purchasing a griddle pan, buy the heaviest and best quality pan you can afford. The manufacturer usually supplies precise instructions on how to care for the griddle pan, so do take time to read and follow these. It is worth your while to take good care of your pan, so that it will give you years of use. Good quality non-stick pans are very easy to wash after use – simply wash in warm soapy water and dry thoroughly. Be especially careful to avoid using harsh scourers or abrasive cleaning materials, otherwise you will damage the non-stick surface. If your pan doesn't have a non-stick surface, fill it with soapy water immediately after you have finished cooking and leave it to soak. This will make it much easier to clean.

FRESH HERBS AND AROMATICS

Fresh herbs and other aromatic plants such as garlic and chillies give wonderful, piquant flavours to griddled dishes – so use them generously to enjoy their special qualities to the full. Nowadays, it is quite easy to buy them at grocer's shops and at large supermarkets. Some herbs are sold in convenient growing pots to keep on your windowsill. If you have space in your garden or window boxes, it is a good idea to grow your own. You can freeze any that are left over in ice cubes to use in sauces and stocks. When it is not possible to get fresh herbs, you can use dried – they will also add excellent flavour to a dish, but they are less aromatic than fresh. Buy dried herbs in small quantities, and use them up as quickly as possible, so that they do not become stale.

You will find the following herbs and aromatic plants very useful:

Basil has bright green leaves which look rather similar to those of mint. It is a very pungent herb which was originally grown in India and is now widely used. It is the main ingredient in pesto, the popular Italian sauce. Basil is also used in salads. It has an intense, spicy aroma and gives a unique flavour to tomato dishes. If you can't grow it in a garden or window box, buy a pot or two of fresh basil and keep it on your window sill.

Chervil has delicate feathery leaves and a mild flavour which is similar to parsley. It also has a hint of aniseed and combines well with fish. It is best used as a subtle garnish, as the leaves are very fragile and wilt quickly when exposed to heat.

Chillies are available in a vast range of flavours, ranging from mild to mouth-searingly hot. Used properly, they can give food a wonderful lift. Some fresh green and red chillies are extremely hot and should be used sparingly, finely chopped and well mixed into the food. Wash your hands immediately after preparing hot chillies, as the juice can cause a burning sensation.

Chives belong to the onion family, and are usually added to dishes just before serving to provide a good, sharp bite of mild green onion flavour. The pretty purple flower heads can also be added to salads.

Coriander has light green, pretty leaves and a fresh peppery flavour. It has a lovely, fresh scent, and is a very useful alternative to parsley. Fresh coriander can be wrapped in clingfilm and stored in the refrigerator for up to about 5 days.

Fennel is a bulbous plant with bright green, feathery leaves. It has a slight flavour of aniseed and the leaves are similar in appearance to dill. Both the bulb and the stalks can be eaten either raw or braised. The bulb is often served as a hot vegetable or raw in salads; the leaves are used as a herb.

Garlic is one of the most indispensable of aromatic plants, adding wonderful flavour to a large variety of foods, including meats, fish and vegetables.

Lavender flowers are sometimes used scattered over griddled meats such as chicken or pork. They are also included in some *herbes de Provence* mixtures for use in chicken and fish dishes.

Lemon balm has the most mild and delicate lemon flavour, so it does not overpower. Use it in salads, with fish and chicken and also in desserts.

Lemon verbena has a much stronger lemony flavour, so use it in the same way as lemon balm, but use it more sparingly.

Marigold petals are so pretty! If you can obtain them easily, do use them to give a wonderful splash of colour to salads. They also make a very pretty garnish.

Marjoram is a pungent herb with small, grey-green leaves and mauve or white flowers. It is very aromatic with a sweet, spicy flavour. It is usually associated with pasta dishes, tomatoes, chicken, fish and vegetable dishes. It is the cultivated version of oregano (see below).

Mint is a refreshingly versatile herb and comes in many different varieties – the most common of which is spearmint. Other delicious flavours available are apple, lemon, pineapple – even ginger mint.

Nasturtium flowers and leaves look colourful and pretty and taste wonderful in salads. The leaves have a distinctive, peppery flavour.

Oregano is wild marjoram. Like the cultivated variety, it is widely used to give flavour to tomato, fish and lamb dishes. Oregano has a stronger flavour than marjoram.

Parsley is available in two varieties – curled and flat-leaf. It is delicious in most savoury dishes. Try the flat-leaved continental variety as a refreshing change from common parsley – it has a much more subtle flavour.

Rocket is a pungent, refreshing salad herb which has become a very popular ingredient in modern salads.

Rosemary is wonderfully aromatic and has a piercingly fresh flavour. It is best suited to lamb or pork dishes. It can also be used with chicken or fish, but use it carefully as the flavour is powerful.

Sage is a green herb with pink or mauve flowers, and leaves that have a grey-green velvety sheen. It is a very aromatic herb with a slightly bitter taste. It is easily available fresh or dried, and gives a rich flavour to pork, veal and chicken dishes.

Tarragon in cooking always means French tarragon (there is a Russian variety but it is virtually flavourless.) Tarragon, with its strong, clear scent and flavour, has a particular affinity with chicken.

Thyme is a small, bushy shrub with grey-green leaves and small pink, mauve, red or white flowers. Thyme has a fragrant aroma and a clove-like taste. It is available in many flavours – including lemon and apple. The classic variety has a delicious, fresh aroma.

MAKING HERB BUTTERS

Herb butters make scrumptious toppings for your griddled fish, meat and vegetable dishes, and they are really easy to make. Use the basic recipe that follows, or vary it according to what herbs you have available. Several examples are provided to give you some general guidelines. However it is great fun to experiment and create your own recipes. The butter should be cool and firm, but not taken straight from the refrigerator.

Parsley Butter
75 g/3 oz butter
1 garlic clove, peeled
3 tablespoons chopped parsley
1 tablespoon lemon juice
salt and pepper

1 Blend the butter in a blender or food processor to soften, then add the remaining ingredients.
2 Chill until firm. Alternatively, pound the butter in a mortar until it is creamy, then add the other ingredients gradually until they are well mixed. Chill until firm.

Variations

Basil Butter: use the same method with 2 tablespoons chopped basil.

Mint Butter: use the same method with 2 tablespoons chopped mint.

Tarragon Butter: use the same method with 2 tablespoons chopped tarragon.

Chive Butter: omit the garlic and use the same method with 2 tablespoons chopped chives.

Mixed Herb Butter: omit the garlic and use the same method with roughly ½ tablespoon chopped tarragon; ½ tablespoon chopped chervil; ½ tablespoon chopped dill; ½ tablespoon chopped chives and ½ tablespoon chopped mint, varying the balance to suit your taste.

MAKING FLAVOURED OILS

Olive oil is the oil most commonly used throughout the book. As olives are grown in many countries, you can buy oil from France, Spain, Italy, Greece, and North Africa. The term 'virgin' on the bottle label simply means that the oil has not been processed using heat or chemicals. Buy the best quality that you can afford, and also try out the various other kinds of cooking oils available on your supermarket shelf. These include sunflower, safflower, sesame seed, walnut, hazelnut, groundnut, pumpkin seed and grapeseed. Grapeseed oil is useful to mix with stronger oils to soften the flavour.

Experiment with different oils to discover which ones you like best.

Making your own flavoured oils will certainly please your taste buds, and they are much more economical than the expensive versions sold in supermarkets. The method for making flavoured oil is very simple. The basic recipes given below use olive oil, but you can vary the oil according to your personal taste.

BASIL OIL

4 tablespoons chopped basil
450 ml/¾ pint olive oil

1 Pound the basil briefly in a mortar. Add a little of the oil and pound again. Add the rest of the oil gradually and pour into a wide-mouthed glass bottle. Seal tightly.
2 Keep the oil for 2 weeks before using, shaking the bottle every 2 or 3 days.

AROMATIC OIL

450 ml/¾ pint olive oil
2 branches rosemary
6 thyme sprigs
1 large garlic clove, peeled and halved
1 green chilli pepper
5–6 small red chilli peppers
6 black peppercorns
6 juniper berries

1 Pour the oil into a clear glass bottle with a tightly-fitting cork. Wash the herbs thoroughly and dry them with kitchen paper.
2 Drop the herbs into the oil with the remaining ingredients. Seal tightly.

3 Keep the oil for 2 weeks before using, shaking the bottle every 2 or 3 days.

Variations
Instead of using chopped herbs, use whole sprigs of rosemary, thyme, or tarragon. They will flavour the oil and look pretty as well. You can also make a spicy chilli oil by gently heating some olive oil with a few dried chillies and leaving to infuse overnight. Strain the oil the next day and transfer to a clear glass bottle with a tight fitting cork.

Starters, Salads and Vegetables

Crisp, new vegetables and firm-textured cheeses such as feta and haloumi can be successfully griddled to make delicious and healthy starters, snacks, side dishes and salads. The griddled ingredients can be served simply tossed in tasty dressings or combined and served with polenta, pasta, rice or breads to make more substantial meals.

Griddled Leeks, Asparagus and Peppers with Balsamic Vinegar

Once you have prepared this, you can leave it for a while to allow all the flavours to combine, then serve at room temperature. Guaranteed to be delicious!

Preparation time: 10 minutes
Cooking time: 15 minutes

- 2 red peppers, cored, deseeded and quartered
- 250 g/8 oz baby leeks
- 250 g/8 oz asparagus
- 3 tablespoons extra virgin olive oil
- 2 tablespoons balsamic vinegar
- 1 bunch of flat leaf parsley, chopped
- sea salt and pepper

1 Heat the griddle pan. Place the red peppers, baby leeks and asparagus on the griddle pan and cook for *5 minutes*, turning them occasionally.

2 Mix all the vegetables with the olive oil, balsamic vinegar, chopped parsley, salt and pepper and serve.

Serves 4

Courgettes and Peppers Griddled with Penne and Brie

Preparation time: 5 minutes
Cooking time: 15 minutes

- 4 courgettes, sliced
- 1 red, 1 green and 1 yellow pepper, cored, deseeded and sliced
- 500 g/1 lb dried penne
- 175 g/6 oz ripe Brie, diced
- 2 tablespoons olive oil
- 1 bunch of dill, chopped
- sea salt and pepper

1 Heat the griddle pan. Place the courgettes and peppers on the griddle pan and cook for *5 minutes*, turning occasionally.

2 Cook the penne for *8 minutes* in lightly salted boiling water. Drain well and return to the pan.

3 Add the griddled vegetables, diced Brie, olive oil and dill to the cooked pasta. Season to taste, mix well over a low heat for *5 minutes* and serve.

Serves 4

variation _____

Griddled Vegetables with Penne and Gorgonzola

Preparation time: 5 minutes
Cooking time: 15 minutes

1 Follow the main recipe substituting 75 g/3 oz of Gorgonzola for the Brie and chopped parsley for the dill.

Serves 4

Spicy Courgette Fritters

These can be served as an accompanying vegetable or, for a really special treat, topped with smoked salmon and cream cheese and served as an appetizer.

Preparation time: 10 minutes
Cooking time: 20 minutes

- 500 g/1 lb courgettes, grated
- 1 egg, beaten
- 2 tablespoons plain flour
- 1 chilli, deseeded and
  chopped
- 1 garlic clove, crushed
- 75 g/3 oz Cheddar cheese,
  grated
- sea salt and pepper
- sprigs of dill, to garnish

1 Heat the griddle pan. Squeeze the excess moisture out of the grated courgettes – the best way to do this is to place all the courgettes into a clean tea towel and squeeze well.

2 Mix together the egg and flour until smooth, add all the other ingredients, mix well and season to taste.

3 Spoon out the mixture on to the griddle, flatten with a palette knife and allow the fritters to cook for *4–5 minutes*. Then turn and cook for a further *4–5 minutes*. Do not disturb them while they are cooking as a crust needs to form on the cooking side, otherwise they will be difficult to turn.

4 Keep the cooked fritters warm and repeat until all the mixture has been used. Serve the fritters between layers of smoked salmon and cream cheese, and garnished with sprigs of dill.

Serves 4

variation _____

Spicy Potato Fritters

Replace the courgettes with potatoes to make another delicious dish that can be served as an accompanying vegetable or as an appetizer.

Preparation time: 10 minutes
Cooking time: 20 minutes

- 500 g/1 lb potatoes, grated
- 1 egg, beaten
- 2 tablespoons plain flour
- 1 chilli, deseeded and
  chopped
- 1 garlic clove, crushed
- 75 g/3 oz Cheddar cheese,
  grated
- sea salt and pepper

1 Heat the griddle pan. Squeeze out any excess moisture from the potatoes as for step 1 of the main recipe.

2 Mix together the egg and flour until smooth, add all the other ingredients, mix well and season to taste.

3 Cook the fritters following step 3 of the main recipe. Keep the cooked fritters warm and repeat until all the mixture has been used.

Serves 4

Chicken Caesar Salad

This makes a great main summer meal and the combination of the classic Caesar salad with griddled chicken breast is just delicious served with some warm crusty bread.

Preparation time: 15 minutes
Cooking time: 20 minutes

- 4 small chicken breasts
- 1 garlic clove, crushed
- 3 anchovy fillets, chopped
- 4 tablespoons lemon juice
- 2 teaspoons mustard powder
- 1 egg yolk
- 200 ml/7 fl oz olive oil
- vegetable oil, for frying

- 3 slices of country bread, cubed
- 1 large Cos lettuce, washed and torn into pieces
- 3 tablespoons freshly grated Parmesan cheese
- sea salt and pepper

1 Heat the griddle pan. Place the chicken breasts on a moderately hot griddle and cook for *10 minutes* on each side.

2 Place the garlic, anchovies, lemon juice, mustard and egg yolk in a small container and, using a whisk or hand-held blender, mix until smooth. Slowly pour in the olive oil and blend until smooth and creamy. If the sauce is too thick, simply add a little water to thin it down. Season to taste with salt and pepper.

3 Heat the vegetable oil in a frying pan and test with a small piece of bread. If the oil sizzles, add the croûtons, turning until golden all over. Remove the croûtons and place them on some kitchen paper to absorb excess oil.

4 Place the lettuce in a bowl, pour over half the dressing and add 2 tablespoons of Parmesan cheese. Mix well.

5 When the chicken breasts are cooked, remove them from the griddle and slice into strips.

6 Divide the lettuce between 4 plates. Sprinkle with the croûtons, arrange the chicken on top, drizzle with the remaining dressing and sprinkle with the remaining Parmesan. Serve at once.

Serves 4

Aubergine and Tabbouleh Salad

The secret of success of this salad is to use a lot of parsley – you just cannot have enough. For something a little different, a mixture of half parsley and half mint makes a refreshing change.

Preparation time: 20 minutes
Cooking time: 15 minutes

- 75 g/3 oz cracked wheat or
  couscous
- 2 aubergines, sliced and
  griddled (see page 19)
- 4 tomatoes, quartered,
  deseeded and sliced
  lengthways

- 3 tablespoons olive oil
- grated rind and juice of
  1 lemon
- 1 large bunch of flat-leaf
  parsley, coarsely chopped
- sea salt and pepper

1 Soak the cracked wheat in water for *15 minutes*, then drain and squeeze out any excess moisture and place in a mixing bowl.

2 Chop the griddled aubergines into small dice.

3 Mix all the ingredients together, season with salt and pepper and serve. This salad is best eaten on the day that it is made and is an ideal accompaniment to lamb kebabs.

Serves 4

Griddled Aubergines with Lemon Pesto

This dish can be made in advance, on the day of eating, but should not be refrigerated.

Preparation time: 10 minutes
Cooking time: 10 minutes

- 4 aubergines, sliced into rounds, or baby aubergines, sliced lengthways
- 1 large bunch of basil
- 75 g/3 oz pine nuts, toasted
- 1 garlic clove
- 75 g/3 oz Parmesan cheese, grated
- grated rind of 2 lemons
- 4 tablespoons lemon juice
- 3 tablespoons olive oil
- sea salt and pepper

1 Heat the griddle pan. Place the aubergines on the pan and cook for *3 minutes* on each side, then remove and arrange on a serving dish. Repeat until all the aubergines are cooked.

2 To make the pesto, place the basil, pine nuts, garlic, Parmesan, lemon rind and juice, olive oil and seasoning in a food processor or blender and blend until smooth.

3 Drizzle the lemon pesto over the aubergines and serve with crusty bread.

Serves 4

variation ————————————————

Griddled Courgettes with Lemon Pesto

Use courgettes instead of aubergines and drizzle with the same scrumptious lemon pesto.

- 4 large courgettes, sliced
- 1 large bunch of basil
- 75 g/3 oz pine nuts, toasted
- 1 garlic clove
- 75 g/3 oz Parmesan cheese, grated
- grated rind of 2 lemons
- 4 tablespoons lemon juice
- 3 tablespoons olive oil
- sea salt and pepper

1 Heat the griddle pan. Place the courgettes on the pan and cook for *2–3 minutes* on each side, then remove and arrange on a serving dish. Repeat until all the courgettes are cooked.

2 To make the pesto, place the basil, pine nuts, garlic, Parmesan, lemon rind and juice, olive oil and seasoning in a food processor or blender and blend until smooth.

3 Drizzle the pesto over the courgettes and serve.

Serves 4

Pear and Stilton Salad

The combination of pear and Stilton, used here to good effect, must have been made in heaven!

Preparation time:10 minutes
Cooking time: 7 minutes

- 4 pears
- 4 tablespoons lemon juice
- 250 g/8 oz baby spinach or mixed salad leaves
- 4 chopped walnuts
- 250 g/8 oz Stilton, crumbled
- 4 tablespoons walnut oil

1 Heat the griddle pan.

2 Cut each pear into quarters and remove the core, then slice each quarter in half. Place the slices of pear on the griddle and cook on each side for *1 minute*. Remove and sprinkle them with the lemon juice.

3 Pile the spinach or mixed salad leaves on a large platter and arrange the pears on top. Sprinkle with the walnuts and crumbled Stilton and spoon the walnut oil over the salad. Serve immediately.

Serves 4

Griddled Asparagus Salad

Trim the ends of each asparagus stalk by cutting across at a sharp angle. Make the cut just where the lovely, bright green colour starts to fade into a dull green.

Preparation time: 15 minutes
Cooking time: about 5 minutes

- **3 tablespoons olive oil (optional)**
- **500 g/1 lb asparagus**
- **125 g/4 oz rocket or other green leaves**
- **2 spring onions, finely sliced**
- **4 radishes, thinly sliced**
- **sea salt and pepper**

TARRAGON AND LEMON DRESSING:

- **2 tablespoons tarragon vinegar**
- **finely grated rind of 1 lemon**
- **¼ teaspoon Dijon mustard**
- **pinch of sugar**
- **1 tablespoon chopped tarragon**
- **5 tablespoons olive oil**
- **sea salt and pepper**

TO GARNISH:

- **coarsely chopped herbs such as tarragon, parsley, chervil and dill**
- **thin strips of lemon rind**

1 To make the dressing put all the dressing ingredients in a screw-top jar and shake well to combine.

2 Heat the oil (if using) in the griddle pan; place the asparagus on the pan in a single layer. Cook for about *5 minutes*, turning occasionally. The asparagus should be tender when pierced with the tip of a sharp knife, and lightly patched with brown. Remove from the pan to a shallow dish and sprinkle with sea salt and pepper. Pour on the tarragon and lemon dressing and toss gently, then leave to cool for *5 minutes*.

3 Arrange the rocket or green leaves on a platter, sprinkle the spring onions and radishes over the top and arrange the asparagus in a pile in the middle of the leaves. Garnish with chopped herbs and thin strips of lemon rind. Serve the salad with bread or as an accompaniment to a main dish.

Serves 4

Griddled Potatoes with Fennel and Olive Oil

This vegetable dish is particularly good served with salmon steaks, since fennel and fish
are a winning combination.

Preparation time: 5 minutes
Cooking time: 30 minutes

- **500 g/1 lb pink new potatoes**
  or blue truffle potatoes,
  halved
- **2 fennel heads, cut into thin**
  wedges

- **a drizzle of olive oil**
- **sea salt and pepper**

1 Heat the griddle pan. Griddle the potatoes for *10 minutes*
on each side or until soft when tested with a knife. Remove
and keep warm – allowing the potatoes to sit for *10 minutes*
to steam in their skins – while you continue to griddle the rest
of the potatoes.

2 Griddle the fennel for *3–4 minutes* on each side. Add to the
cooked potatoes, drizzle with olive oil and season well.

Serves 4

Coriander and New Potato Salad with Yogurt Dressing

This is a simple potato salad has a slightly unusual dressing and is both refreshing and healthy. It makes a good accompaniment to trout or a similar fish. Mint could be substituted for the coriander if preferred.

Preparation time: 8 minutes, plus standing
Cooking time: 22 minutes

- 750 g/1½ lb new potatoes, halved lengthways
- 1 large bunch of coriander
- 4 tablespoons natural yogurt
- 1 tablespoon olive oil
- 4 tablespoons lemon juice
- 1 garlic clove, crushed
- a few drops of Tabasco sauce
- sea salt and pepper

1 Heat the griddle pan to a low heat. Place the potatoes on the griddle. Cook on each side for *10 minutes*, then allow to stand for approximately *10 minutes,* to allow them to steam in their skins.

2 Roughly chop the coriander, reserving some for the garnish. Combine the chopped coriander with the yogurt, olive oil, lemon juice, garlic and Tabasco sauce. Season to taste with salt and pepper and mix well. Add the potatoes to the dressing and stir in.

3 Serve immediately or allow to cool. Garnish with the reserved coriander before serving.

Serves 4

Griddling Extras

The art of good cooking lies in a store cupboard well stocked with basic ingredients and staples and griddling is no exception. Many spices and flavourings are used to enhance the flavour of griddled food, and polenta, various pastas and breads are ideal accompaniments.

Polenta

Sesame seeds

Mixed peppercorns

Juniper berries

Dried red chillies

Violet olives

Buckwheat

Polenta is a yellow ground maize with a nutty flavour. Mix it with water or stock, butter and Parmesan and serve as an accompaniment to griddled vegetables, poultry or meat.
Sesame seeds are commonly used in stir-fries and salad dressings and are the source of sesame seed oil.
Dried red chillies are a widely used spice, which add an intense fiery flavour to food, oils or vinegar.
Mixed peppercorns are the dried berry-like fruit from a tropical vine. They are crushed to form a pungent spice; the different colours represent the different stages of ripeness of the fruit.
Violet olives are the fruit of an evergreen tree native to the Mediterranean. As the olives ripen their colour changes from green through to violet then black when fully ripe.
Juniper berries are dried berries from the evergreen juniper bush. They are used in sauces and marinades and crushed for use as a coating for griddled meats.
Buckwheat is a dark coloured grain from a cereal plant originally from the Orient.

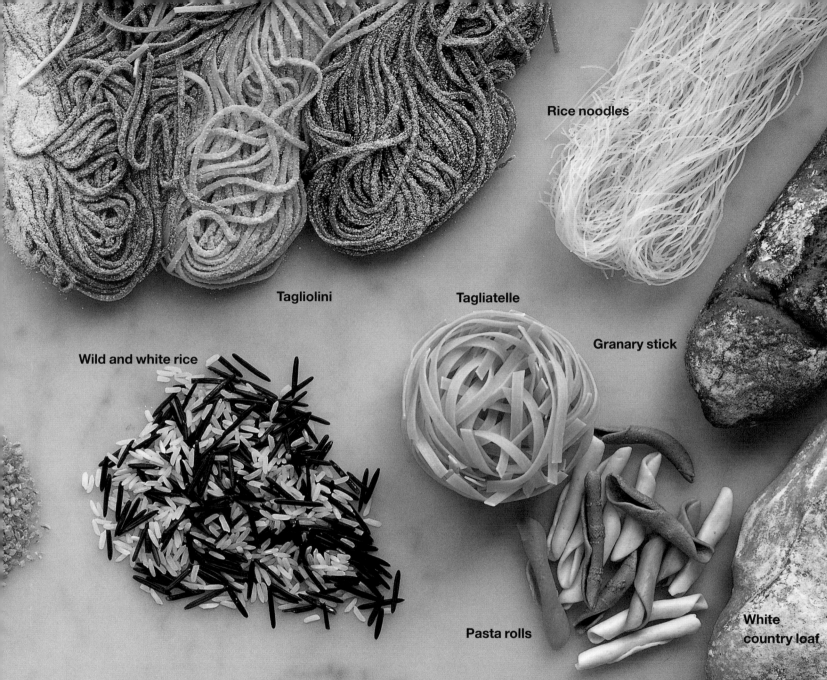

Rice noodles

Tagliolini

Tagliatelle

Wild and white rice

Granary stick

Pasta rolls

White country loaf

Its seeds are roasted and made into flour used in pancakes and pasta. **Tagliolini**, also called tagliarini, is a shorter and thinner form of tagliatelle. It is available fresh or dried, flavoured with spinach and sun-dried tomatoes.

Wild and white rice derive from semi-aquatic grass in warm climates. White rice is the inner kernel, when cleaned and husked. **Rice noodles** are long narrow strings or flat strips originally from Asia, which are supposed to signify long life.

Tagliatelle is a flat wide pasta which is ideal for serving with griddled poultry and meat. **Pasta rolls** flavoured with spinach and sun-dried tomatoes provide an interesting alternative to traditional forms of pasta. **Granary stick** is made from

brown flour including the wholewheat grain. It is coarser than white flour and therefore more nutritious. **White country loaf** is made from wheat flour; the wheat bran and germ have been removed to leave a smooth even texture and colour.

Griddled and Baked Open Vegetable Tart with Parmesan

This is both delicious and easy, and various vegetables can be used, as you prefer. It is very good eaten either hot or cold on a warm summer's day with a green salad.

Preparation time: 20 minutes
Cooking time: 20 minutes
Oven temperature: 200°C (400°F), Gas Mark 6

- 1 red onion
- 1 red pepper
- 1 leek
- 2 flat mushrooms
- 1 small fennel bulb
- 1 small aubergine or 4 baby aubergines
- 1 courgette
- 2 garlic cloves, peeled but left whole
- 1 bunch of basil

- a drizzle of olive oil
- 75 g/3 oz Parmesan, coarsely grated
- sea salt and pepper

PASTRY:
- 175 g/6 oz self raising flour
- 50 g/2 oz butter, softened
- 1 teaspoon dried mixed herbs
- 75 ml/3 fl oz water
- 75 ml/3 fl oz olive oil

1 Griddle all the vegetables before making the pastry: cut them into wedges or halves and griddle until lightly patched with black. Griddle the garlic cloves whole and then slice.

2 For the pastry, mix together the flour and butter in a food processor or by hand until all the butter is mixed in. Add the herbs, water and oil, and mix to form a dough ball. Knead the dough on a lightly floured work surface until smooth.

3 Lightly oil a baking sheet and gently press the dough out to form a circle about 25–30 cm/10–12 inches in diameter.

4 Arrange the griddled vegetables over the dough, pressing them in gently. Strip the leaves from the basil, then press them into the dough. Drizzle with olive oil, season well and sprinkle with Parmesan. Bake in a preheated oven, 200°C (400°F), Gas Mark 6, for *12–15 minutes*, until the dough is risen and golden.

Serves 4–6

Warm Salad of Griddled Beetroot and Parsnips

Beetroot and parsnips go together surprisingly well, as well as making an attractive visual contrast.

Preparation time: 10 minutes
Cooking time: 20 minutes

- 500 g/1 lb raw beetroot, peeled and cut into 1 cm/½ inch thick slices
- 500 g/1 lb parsnips, peeled and cut into 1 cm/½ inch thick slices
- 4 tablespoons soured cream
- 3 tablespoons water
- 1 bunch of dill, chopped
- sea salt and pepper

1 Heat the griddle pan. Griddle the beetroot slices on each side for *4–5 minutes*, remove and keep warm. Repeat until all the slices are cooked.

2 Then griddle the slices of parsnip on each side for *4–5 minutes*, remove and add to the beetroot. Repeat until all the slices are cooked.

3 Mix together the soured cream, water, dill and seasoning, and drizzle over the griddled beetroot and parsnips. This is another salad ideal for serving with fish.

Serves 4

Griddled Beetroot, Feta and Trevise Salad

Trevise is a member of the chicory family, which is common in Italy and has a slightly bitter taste. It is now found more easily here than it used to be. If you cannot find any trevise, you can use chicory or rocket instead.

Preparation time: 10 minutes
Cooking time: 10 minutes

- 500 g/1 lb raw beetroot, peeled and cut into 1 cm/½ inch thick slices
- 1 large head or 250 g/8 oz trevise
- 1 tablespoon red wine vinegar
- 2 tablespoons extra virgin olive oil
- 1 bunch of flat leaf parsley, chopped
- 250 g/8 oz feta cheese
- sea salt and pepper

1 Heat the griddle pan. Place the beetroot slices on the griddle and cook on each side for *4–5 minutes.*

2 Cut the trevise into wedges, remove the hard core and place on the griddle to cook until just wilted, then remove and add to the beetroot.

3 Add the vinegar, olive oil and chopped parsley to the beetroot and trevise. Season to taste and toss well. Place in a serving dish, crumble the feta over the top and serve.

Serves 4

Griddled Vegetables with Creamed Polenta

Polenta is a cornmeal porridge traditionally eaten in northern Italy. It is very versatile and can be used for many different dishes.

Preparation time: 15 minutes
Cooking time: 20 minutes

- 1 red pepper, cored, deseeded and quartered
- 4 baby aubergines, quartered
- 4 baby courgettes, quartered
- 8 baby sweetcorn
- 8 baby leeks
- 1 red onion, cut into wedges, root left intact
- 8 baby tomatoes
- 600 ml/1 pint water
- 150 g/5 oz instant polenta flour
- 50 g/2 oz butter, plus a little extra for greasing
- 2 tablespoons olive oil, plus a little extra for drizzling
- 1 bunch of oregano, chopped
- 175 g/6 oz rindless soft goats' cheese
- sea salt and pepper

1 Heat the griddle pan and griddle all the vegetables for *2–4 minutes* on each side. Keep warm in a large dish.

2 Heat the water to a gentle boil, pour in the polenta and beat well for *1–2 minutes* until it becomes a smooth paste. Reduce the heat and cook the polenta for *6–8 minutes* until it thickens, stirring constantly so that it does not catch on the bottom of the pan.

3 Add the butter, olive oil and oregano, and season to taste with salt and pepper. Mix well. The polenta should be the consistency of soft mashed potatoes.

4 Grease a large serving dish with butter, spread the polenta over the bottom of it and arrange the griddled vegetables on top. Crumble the goats' cheese over the top, drizzle with olive oil and place under a hot grill until the cheese has melted. Serve with a leafy salad if liked.

Serves 4

variation
Griddled Vegetables with Tagliatelle

This dish can be served hot in winter, but in summer it is very good served cold as a salad with griddled meat or fish.

Preparation time: 10 minutes
Cooking time: 20 minutes

- 1 red pepper, cored, deseeded and quartered
- 4 baby aubergines, quartered
- 4 baby courgettes, quartered
- 8 baby sweetcorn
- 8 baby leeks
- 1 red onion, cut into wedges, root left intact
- 8 baby tomatoes
- 500 g/1 lb fresh tagliatelle
- 4 tablespoons olive oil
- 175 g/6 oz rindless soft goats' cheese
- 1 bunch of oregano, chopped
- sea salt and pepper

1 Griddle all the vegetables as for step 1 of the main recipe.

2 Bring a saucepan of water to the boil, immerse the pasta in it and cook for *4 minutes*. Then drain and toss in the olive oil. Season to taste.

3 Add the warm griddled vegetables, crumble in the goats' cheese and the oregano. Mix together well and serve.

Serves 4

Griddled Vegetable Risotto

If you love the taste of griddled vegetables and risotto, this dish is for you! The vegetables can be altered according to what you find in the shops or in your kitchen.

Preparation time: 10 minutes
Cooking time: 30 minutes

- 1 red onion, sliced
- 125 g/4 oz asparagus, chopped
- 2 courgettes, sliced
- 4 mushrooms, sliced
- 125 g/4 oz butternut pumpkin, diced
- 1 litre/1¾ pints vegetable or chicken stock
- 125 g/4 oz butter

- 1 tablespoon olive oil
- 1 garlic clove, crushed
- 1 onion, finely chopped
- 300 g/10 oz arborio rice
- 75 ml/3 fl oz dry white wine
- 1 tablespoon chopped sage
- 125 g/4 oz Parmesan, grated
- 1 tablespoon chopped sage, to garnish

1 Heat the griddle pan and griddle all the vegetables, cooking them for about *5 minutes*, turning occasionally and cooking in batches if necessary.

2 Meanwhile, make the risotto. Pour the stock into a saucepan and simmer.

3 Heat half the butter and the oil in a heavy-based saucepan, add the garlic and chopped onion and cook for *2 minutes*. Do not allow to brown.

4 Add the arborio rice to the pan, stirring well to coat the grains with the butter mixture, and pour in enough hot stock to cover the rice. Stir the rice frequently and simmer gently, gradually adding the remaining stock as it evaporates. Test the rice after *18 minutes* and, if it is not cooked, cook for a little longer, still stirring so that it does not stick on the bottom of the pan.

5 Add the white wine, sage, Parmesan, griddled onion, asparagus, courgettes, mushrooms and pumpkin and the remaining butter. Mix well and cook for *3 minutes* – the risotto should have a creamy texture – then serve, garnished with Parmesan shavings and chopped sage.

Serves 4

Griddled Haloumi Cheese with Beef Tomatoes

Haloumi is a sheep's milk cheese with a firm texture similar to feta, which griddles very successfully.

Preparation time: 15 minutes
Cooking time: 20 minutes

- 2 packets of haloumi cheese
- 1 bag of mixed lettuce
- 2 tablespoons olive oil
- 4 tablespoons lemon juice
- 1 bunch of marjoram, chopped

- 4 beef tomatoes, skinned, cored and cut into wedges
- 75 g/3 oz pitted olives (optional)
- sea salt and pepper

1 Heat the griddle pan. Cut the haloumi into 16 slices and place on the griddle to cook for *3–4 minutes* on each side.

2 Arrange the lettuce on 4 serving plates.

3 Mix together the olive oil, lemon juice and marjoram, and season to taste with salt and pepper.

4 Arrange the haloumi and tomato wedges alternately on the lettuce. Add the olives, if using, and spoon over the dressing. Serve immediately, while the cheese is still warm.

Serves 4

Bruschetta with Griddled Pepper, Garlic and Parmesan

Preparation time: 10 minutes
Cooking time: 15 minutes

- 4 red peppers
- 1 sprig of rosemary, very finely chopped
- 125 g/4 oz Parmesan cheese shavings
- a drizzle of olive oil
- 4 large slices of country bread or other crusty loaf, thickly cut
- 2 garlic cloves, peeled
- sea salt and pepper
- rosemary leaves, to garnish

1 Heat the griddle pan and griddle all the peppers until the skin is charred. Peel the skin from the peppers and chop up roughly. Add the rosemary and half the Parmesan shavings, and season to taste. Mix well with a little olive oil.

2 Toast or griddle the bread on both sides. Rub one side of the bread with the garlic cloves and drizzle with olive oil.

3 Heat the grill. Place the prepared toast on a baking sheet, spoon the pepper mix on to the bread and spread evenly. Sprinkle with the remaining Parmesan shavings and place under the grill for a few minutes or until sizzling.

4 Serve garnished with the rosemary leaves, as an appetizer or as part of a main meal with griddled fish, if liked.

Serves 4

variation
Bruschetta with Griddled Aubergines, Tomatoes and Goats' Cheese

The goats' cheese adds a burst of flavour to the aubergines and tomatoes.

Preparation time: 10 minutes
Cooking time: 15 minutes

- 2 aubergines, sliced
- 2 tomatoes, halved
- 1 bunch of basil, chopped
- 125 g/4 oz creamy rindless goats' cheese, crumbled
- a drizzle of olive oil
- 4 large slices of country bread, thickly cut
- 2 garlic cloves, peeled
- sea salt and pepper

1 Heat the griddle pan and griddle the aubergines and tomatoes for *5 minutes*, turning occasionally. When cooked, chop them up roughly, add the basil and half the goats' cheese. Season to taste and mix well with a little olive oil.

2 Toast or griddle the bread on both sides. Rub one side of the bread with the garlic cloves and drizzle with olive oil. Place the prepared toast on a baking sheet, spoon the aubergine mix on top and spread evenly. Sprinkle with the remaining goats' cheese and place under a preheated grill for a few minutes or until sizzling.

Serves 4

Bruschetta with Griddled Mushrooms and Ricotta

Large flat field mushrooms are the best choice for this recipe.

Preparation time: 5 minutes
Cooking time: 15 minutes

- 4 large flat field mushrooms, stalks removed
- 4 slices of country bread, thickly cut
- 2 garlic cloves, peeled
- a drizzle of olive oil
- 1 small bag of baby spinach leaves
- 125 g/4 oz ricotta cheese
- sea salt and pepper

1 Heat the griddle pan and griddle the mushrooms for *3–4 minutes* on each side.

2 Heat the grill and toast the bread. Rub one side of the toast generously with the garlic and drizzle with olive oil.

3 Place the toast on a baking sheet. Divide the spinach between the pieces of toast, place a mushroom on top and spoon on some ricotta cheese.

4 Season with salt and pepper and grill for *3–4 minutes*. Serve either hot or at room temperature.

Serves 4

Focaccia Sandwich with Mediterranean Vegetables and Mozzarella

This sandwich makes a whole meal in itself. It can be prepared in advance and then wrapped in clingfilm and eaten on your travels.

Preparation time: 10 minutes
Cooking time: 20 minutes

- 1 small aubergine, sliced
- 2 courgettes, sliced lengthways
- 1 red onion, sliced into rings
- 1 loaf of focaccia bread
- 1 garlic clove, halved (optional)
- 1 packet of mozzarella cheese, sliced
- 2 red peppers, griddled and skinned (see page 34)
- 75 g/3 oz rocket
- a drizzle of olive oil
- sea salt and pepper

1 Heat the griddle pan and griddle the aubergine, courgettes and red onion for about *5 minutes*, turning occasionally. Leave to cool.

2 Cut the focaccia in half lengthways and place on the griddle to toast lightly. Rub the cut garlic edges all over the toasted bread. Place the sliced mozzarella on the base of the toasted focaccia.

3 Evenly layer the griddled vegetables on top of the mozzarella. Start with the aubergine and then add the courgettes, peppers, onion and rocket. Season each layer as you arrange it.

4 Finally, drizzle with a little olive oil, season and place the top of the focaccia bread on top of the vegetables. Push together gently but firmly.

5 Cut into 4 even-sized pieces and serve.

Serves 4

Griddled Polenta Salad with Goats' Cheese and Chilli Oil

Chilli oil can be bought, but you can easily make it yourself – just add chillies and garlic to olive oil and leave to marinate for at least 1 week. The amount of added ingredients can be varied according to taste.

Preparation time: 15 minutes
Cooking time: 15–20 minutes

- 600 ml/1 pint water
- 150 g/5 oz instant polenta flour
- 25 g/1 oz butter
- 250 g/8 oz rindless creamy goats' cheese
- 1 small radicchio, quartered
- 125 g/4 oz rocket or watercress
- 3 tablespoons chilli oil
- 1 tablespoon balsamic vinegar
- sea salt and pepper
- rocket leaves, to garnish

1 Heat the water until gently simmering, pour in the polenta flour and beat well until it becomes a smooth paste. Reduce the heat and continue to cook, stirring constantly, for *3–4 minutes* until it thickens.

2 When it is thick and cooked, add the butter, season with salt and pepper, and mix well.

3 Place the polenta on a chopping board and spread until it is 2.5 cm/1 inch thick. Allow to set for *5 minutes*.

4 Heat the griddle pan and the grill.

5 Spread or crumble the goats' cheese over the polenta, and cut into fingers about 2.5 x 7cm/1 x 3 inches.

6 Griddle the radicchio for *2–3 minutes* on each side. Arrange on a plate with the rocket.

7 Place the fingers of polenta on the griddle and cook for *7–8 minutes.* Grill the polenta for *3 minutes*, just to melt the goats' cheese, then arrange it on top of the lettuce, drizzle over the chilli oil and balsamic vinegar, and season well. Garnish with rocket leaves.

Serves 4

Fish

Griddling is an ideal way of cooking fish and shellfish. Not only is it very easy, but it also results in an attractive finish for fish with the distinctive scorch marks on the flesh. Already a low-fat food, when griddled fish makes an even healthier meal, ideally served with a crisp salad or lightly steamed seasonal vegetables. Many herbs marry well with fish and herb butters make scrumptious toppings for griddled fish.

Salmon wrapped in Parma Ham with Fontina Cheese and Bay Leaves

Preparation time: 10 minutes
Cooking time: 10 minutes

- 4 x 175 g/6 oz salmon fillets, skinned
- 4 thin slices of Fontina cheese
- 4 or 8 bay leaves, depending on size
- 8 thin slices of Parma ham
- sea salt and pepper
- fresh pasta or mixed salad leaves, to serve

1 Heat the griddle pan. Season the salmon fillets to taste.

2 Trim any rind from the Fontina cheese and cut to fit on top of the salmon fillets. Place the cheese slices on the salmon fillets, then place the bay leaves on top of the cheese and wrap the Parma ham around the salmon, securing the cheese and bay leaves.

3 Cook the prepared salmon fillets on the griddle for *4–5 minutes* on each side, taking care when turning.

4 Serve with fresh pasta tossed in butter, or a leafy salad.

Serves 4

variation ———————————————

Cod wrapped in Parma Ham with Gruyère Cheese

Preparation time: 10 minutes
Cooking time: 10 minutes

- 4 x 175 g/6 oz cod fillets, skinned
- 4 thin slices of Gruyère or Emmenthal cheese
- 4 or 8 bay leaves, depending on size
- 8 thin slices of Parma ham
- sea salt and pepper

1 Heat the griddle pan. Season the cod fillets to taste.

2 Trim any rind from the cheese and cut it to fit on top of the cod fillets. Place the cheese slices on the fish, then place the bay leaves on top of the cheese and wrap the Parma ham around the cod, securing the cheese and bay leaves.

3 Cook the cod on the griddle for *4–5 minutes* on each side, taking care when turning each fillet. Serve with a leafy salad.

Serves 4

Griddled Monkfish with Leeks and Parmesan

This dish has a wonderful crunchy coating around the firm monkfish slices. The quantity can be halved and served as an appetizer, but it is so popular that it is a good idea to make the full amount and serve it as finger food with a glass of chilled wine on a summer's evening in the garden.

Preparation time: 10 minutes
Cooking time: 10 minutes

- 1 leek, finely sliced
- 125 g/4 oz Parmesan
  cheese, finely grated
- 750 g/1½ lb prepared
  monkfish fillets, sliced about
  1.5 cm/¾ inch thick

- 1 egg white, lightly beaten
- sea salt and pepper
- lemon wedges, to serve

1 Heat the griddle pan.

2 Mix together the leek and Parmesan and season to taste.

3 Pat the pieces of monkfish dry with kitchen paper. Dip the monkfish into the egg white, and roll in the leek and Parmesan. Place the monkfish on the griddle and cook for *3–4 minutes* on each side. Serve with the lemon wedges.

Serves 4

Griddled Snapper with Red Onions and Thyme

Preparation time: 5 minutes
Cooking time: 15 minutes

- 2 red onions, sliced
- 1 bunch of thyme, chopped
- 4 x 175 g/6 oz snapper fillets
- a drizzle of olive oil
- sea salt and pepper

1 Heat the griddle pan and griddle the slices of red onion until soft. Add the chopped thyme and push the onion to the side of the griddle.

2 Add the snapper fillets and cook for *4 minutes* on each side. Serve with the onions and thyme, drizzle with olive oil and season well.

Serves 4

Griddled Salmon with a Chilli Crust

The chilli crust not only looks good but also imparts some delicious flavours to the fish.

Preparation time: 10 minutes
Cooking time: 10 minutes

- **3 teaspoons crushed dried chillies**
- **8 teaspoons sesame seeds**
- **1 large bunch of parsley, chopped**
- **4 x 150 g/5 oz salmon fillets, skinned**
- **1 egg white, lightly beaten**
- **sea salt and pepper**

TO SERVE:

- **1 lime, cut into wedges and griddled, to serve**
- **noodles**

1 Heat the griddle pan.

2 Mix together the crushed dried chillies, sesame seeds, parsley, salt and pepper, and spread out on a flat plate.

3 Dip the salmon fillets in the egg white. Then coat them in the mixed crust ingredients. Pat the mix on to the salmon to ensure an even covering.

4 Place on the hot griddle pan and cook for *4 minutes* on each side, turning carefully with a palette knife and keeping the crust on the fish. When cooked, remove and serve with the griddled lime quarters and noodles, if liked.

Serves 4

variation _____

Griddled Cod with a Chilli Crust

A good alternative is cod, which absorbs flavours especially well.

Preparation time: 10 minutes
Cooking time: 10 minutes

- **2 teaspoons crushed dried chillies**
- **4 teaspoons sesame seeds**
- **1 bunch of parsley, chopped**
- **4 x 150 g/5 oz cod fillets, skinned**
- **1 egg white, lightly beaten**
- **sea salt and pepper**

TO SERVE:

- **1 lime, cut into wedges and griddled, to serve**
- **noodles**

1 Heat the griddle pan.

2 Prepare and cook the cod fillets following steps 2–4 of the main recipe.

Serves 4

Griddled Snapper with Carrots and Caraway Seeds

Preparation time: 10 minutes
Cooking time: 10 minutes

- 500 g/1 lb carrots, sliced
- 2 teaspoons caraway seeds
- 4 x 175 g/6 oz snapper fillets
- 2 oranges
- 1 bunch of coriander leaves, roughly chopped, plus extra to garnish
- 4 tablespoons olive oil
- sea salt and pepper

1 Heat the griddle pan and griddle the carrots for *3 minutes* on each side, adding the caraway seeds for the last *2 minutes* of cooking. Remove from the griddle and keep warm.

2 Cook the snapper fillets on the griddle for *3 minutes* on each side.

3 Juice one of the oranges and cut the other into quarters. Place the orange quarters on the griddle until browned.

4 Add the coriander to the carrots and mix well. Season to taste and add the olive oil and orange juice. Serve the carrots with the cooked fish and griddled orange wedges. Garnish with the extra chopped coriander.

Serves 4

Mushroom-Stuffed Griddled Halibut Wrapped in Bacon

Preparation time: 15 minutes
Cooking time: 10 minutes

- 1 garlic clove, crushed
- 75 g/3 oz mushrooms, sliced
- 1 small bunch of parsley, chopped
- 2 tablespoons olive oil
- 4 x 175 g/6 oz thick halibut fillets

- 8 slices of rindless streaky bacon
- sea salt and pepper

TO SERVE:

- fresh pasta
- wilted spinach

1 Mix together the garlic, mushrooms, parsley and olive oil, and season to taste.

2 Take the halibut fillets and make a slit in the side of the fillet with a sharp knife. Continue to cut away, to make a pocket.

3 Place the mushroom stuffing in the pocket, compressing it as much as possible.

4 Take the bacon and wrap it around the halibut, using the bacon to help seal up the opening containing the stuffing.

5 Heat the griddle pan. Place the halibut on the griddle and cook for *5 minutes* on each side. Serve the fish with pasta and wilted spinach.

Serves 4

Griddled Halibut with Griddled Mixed Baby Tomatoes

Preparation time: 5 minutes
Cooking time: 15 minutes

- 500 g/1 lb mixed baby tomatoes (such as plum and cherry)
- 4 tablespoons olive oil
- 2 tablespoons balsamic vinegar
- 4 x 175 g/6 oz halibut fillets or steaks
- 1 bunch of green or purple basil
- sea salt and pepper

1 Heat the griddle pan. Place the whole tomatoes on the griddle and cook for about *6 minutes*, rolling them around to cook all over. Some of the tomatoes will split and become very soft. Remove from the griddle, pour the olive oil and balsamic vinegar over the tomatoes, season to taste with salt and pepper, and keep warm.

2 Place the halibut fillets on the hot griddle pan and cook for about *4–6 minutes* on each side, according to the thickness of the fish.

3 Add the basil leaves to the griddled tomato mix and place on 4 plates. Arrange the fish on top, drizzle with a little olive oil and balsamic vinegar, season to taste and serve.

Serves 4

variation ——————————————

Griddled Monkfish and Mixed Baby Tomatoes

This dish is delicious served with fresh soft pasta, lightly tossed in olive oil and seasoning.

Preparation time: 5 minutes
Cooking time: 20 minutes

- 500 g/1 lb mixed baby tomatoes (such as plum and cherry)
- 4 tablespoons olive oil
- 2 tablespoons balsamic vinegar
- 4 x 175 g/6 oz monkfish fillets
- sea salt and pepper

1 Griddle the tomatoes following step 1 of the main recipe.

2 Place the monkfish fillets on the hot griddle pan and cook for about *5–7 minutes* on each side, according to the thickness of the fish.

3 Place the griddled tomatoes on 4 plates and arrange the fish on top, drizzle with a little olive oil and balsamic vinegar, season and serve.

Serves 4

Griddled Cod Steaks with Mint Pesto

It is good to see a fantastic fish like cod cooked in such a simple and fresh way. The mint pesto is delicious and is best made fresh since, although it will keep, it tends to lose its colour and depth of flavour.

Preparation time: 10 minutes
Cooking time: 8–10 minutes

- 4 x 175g/6 oz cod steaks
- steamed green vegetables, to serve
- 1 lime, cut into wedges, to garnish

MINT PESTO:
- 6 tablespoons chopped mint
- 1 tablespoon chopped parsley
- 1 garlic clove, crushed

- 1 tablespoon freshly grated Parmesan cheese
- 1 tablespoon double cream
- 1 teaspoon balsamic vinegar
- 3 tablespoons extra virgin olive oil
- sea salt and pepper
- steamed green vegetables, to serve

1 Heat the griddle pan, put on the cod steaks and cook for *4 minutes* on each side, until the fish is slightly charred and firm to the touch.

2 Place the pesto ingredients in a food processor or blender and process until smooth. Transfer to a small bowl. Serve the cod steaks with a spoonful of pesto and with seasonal steamed green vegetables. Garnish with lime wedges.

Serves 4

Tuna Escalope Sandwich with Spinach, Ricotta and Olive Filling

These open sandwiches are great made with fresh tuna and served on a summer's evening as a quick supper dish with a glass of chilled white wine.

Preparation time: 10 minutes
Cooking time: 10 minutes

- 75 g/3 oz pitted olives
- 1 garlic clove, crushed
- 1 bunch of basil
- 1 tablespoon balsamic vinegar
- 3 tablespoons olive oil
- 4 x 175 g/6 oz tuna steaks
- 4 slices of granary or rye bread
- 125 g/4 oz ricotta cheese
- 1 small bag of baby spinach leaves
- sea salt and pepper
- lemon wedges, to serve

1 Heat the griddle pan.

2 Place the olives, garlic, basil, vinegar and olive oil in a food processor or blender and process. Alternatively, chop by hand and mix together.

3 Place the tuna escalopes on the hot griddle and cook for *1–2 minutes* on each side.

4 Toast the bread, spread with the ricotta cheese, top with generous amounts of spinach and season well. Place the tuna on top of the spinach and top with the green sauce. Season to taste and serve with lemon wedges. Alternatively, cut the toast and tuna escalopes in half and arrange as shown here.

Serves 4

Marinated Ginger and Garlic Green Prawns

These prawns are delicious and make an impressive, if expensive, dish. If you buy the prawns from a fishmonger, he should have a good stock of various sizes.

Preparation time: 20 minutes, plus marinating
Cooking time: 10 minutes

- 24 raw tiger or raw green prawns, peeled, heads removed and deveined
- 5 cm/2 inch piece of fresh root ginger, peeled and finely diced
- 4 large garlic cloves, crushed
- 1 green chilli, deseeded and finely chopped
- 1 bunch of spring onions, cut into 5 cm/2 inch lengths
- 150 g/5 oz rice noodles
- 1 tablespoon sesame oil
- 2 tablespoons soy sauce
- 1 bunch of coriander, chopped
- grated rind and juice of 1 lime
- sea salt and pepper

1 Place the prepared prawns in a glass dish. Add the ginger, garlic and chilli to the prawns, mix well and leave to marinate in the refrigerator for at least *2 hours*. If time is short, marinate them for *1 hour* and do not put them in the refrigerator.

2 Cut the spring onions lengths into thin strips. Place in iced water, where they will become curly – the longer they are left and the colder the water, the curlier they will become.

3 Heat the griddle pan. Put the prawns on the griddle and cook for *3 minutes* on each side.

4 Bring a saucepan of lightly salted water to the boil, add the rice noodles and cook for *2 minutes*. Drain well, then add the sesame oil, soy sauce, coriander, lime rind and juice, and salt and pepper to taste, and toss well.

5 Add the drained spring onions to the prawns, cook for *30 seconds* and arrange on a bed of noodles.

Serves 4

variation _____

Marinated Ginger and Garlic Chicken

Preparation time: 20 minutes, plus marinating
Cooking time: 20 minutes

- 4 small chicken breasts, cut into thin strips
- 5 cm/2 inch piece of fresh root ginger, peeled and finely diced
- 4 large garlic cloves, crushed
- 1 green chilli, deseeded and finely chopped
- 1 bunch of spring onions, cut into 5 cm/2 inch lengths
- 150 g/5 oz rice noodles
- 1 tablespoon sesame oil
- 2 tablespoons soy sauce
- 1 bunch of coriander, chopped
- grated rind and juice of 1 lime
- sea salt and pepper

1 Marinate the chicken following step 1 of the main recipe and prepare the spring onions as in step 2.

2 Heat the griddle pan. Put the chicken on the griddle and cook for *7 minutes* on each side.

3 Complete the recipe following steps 4 and 5 of the main recipe, replacing the prawns with the chicken.

Serves 4

Griddled Tiger Prawns with Mint and Lemon

Preparation time: 10 minutes, plus marinating
Cooking time: 4–6 minutes

- 750 g/1½ lb tiger raw prawns
  peeled, heads removed and
  deveined
- 1 large bunch of mint,
  chopped

- 2 garlic cloves, crushed
- 8 tablespoons lemon juice
- sea salt and pepper
- mint leaves, to garnish

1 Place the prawns in a glass mixing bowl.

2 Add the mint, garlic and lemon juice to the prawns, season to taste and allow to marinate for *30 minutes* or overnight.

3 Heat the griddle pan. Place the prawns and marinade on the griddle, cook on each side for *2–3 minutes* and serve garnished with mint leaves.

Serves 4

Griddled New Zealand Green-Lipped Mussels with Garlic Butter

Green-lipped mussels are usually sold ready-cooked in their half shells and are available from good fishmongers. If you are unable to find green-lipped mussels then use ordinary mussels.

Preparation time: 10 minutes
Cooking time: 5-6 minutes

- 2 garlic cloves, crushed
- 125 g/4 oz butter, softened
- 1 bunch of parsley, chopped
- 24 ready-cooked green-lipped mussels
- sea salt and pepper

1 Heat the griddle pan.

2 Mix the crushed garlic into the softened butter, together with the parsley and seasoning.

3 Spread the butter over the mussel halves with a palette knife, and place on the griddle, shell side on the pan.

4 Allow the mussels to cook for *5–6 minutes* or until all the butter has melted. Serve with crusty country bread to mop up all the juices.

Serves 4

Seared Scallops on Mixed Leaves with Lime Dressing

Scallops go particularly well with the citrus tang of a lime dressing and warm crusty bread.

Preparation time: 10 minutes
Cooking time: 6 minutes

- 16 large scallops, cleaned
- grated rind and juice of
  2 limes
- 3 tablespoons olive oil
- 1 bunch of dill, chopped
- sea salt and pepper
- 1 large bag of your favourite
  mixed leaves, to serve

1 Heat the griddle pan. Dry the scallops well with kitchen paper to remove excess water.

2 Place the scallops on the hot griddle and cook for *3 minutes* on each side.

3 Mix together the lime juice and rind, olive oil and chopped dill, and season with salt and pepper to taste.

4 Toss the salad in the lime dressing and arrange on 4 plates. Place the scallops on the salad; garnish with a little dressing.

Serves 4

Griddled Lobster Tails with Oregano Butter

This dish is expensive and therefore definitely for that special evening. Make sure you go to a good fishmonger for the lobster tails.

Preparation time: 15 minutes
Cooking time: 10 minutes

- 125 g/4 oz butter, softened and cut into small knobs
- 1 large bunch of oregano, chopped
- 4 headless lobster tails, halved lengthways
- sea salt and pepper
- 2 lemons, cut into wedges, to serve

1 Place the butter and oregano in a bowl, mix together and season to taste with salt and pepper. Place the butter in a rough sausage shape on some greaseproof paper, roll and twist the ends tightly and place in the freezer to chill and harden for *10 minutes.*

2 Heat the griddle pan, place the lobster tails on the griddle and cook for *5 minutes* on each side. The shell will turn bright pink and the flesh white.

3 Place the lemons on the griddle for *3 minutes* to colour up and warm the lemon juice.

4 Serve the lobsters with the lemon wedges and accompanied by a salad and new potatoes. Remove the oregano butter from the freezer. Slice and arrange on top of the cooked lobsters to serve.

Serves 4

Griddled Thai Prawn Cakes

These are fish cakes with a difference!

Preparation time: 15 minutes
Cooking time: 15 minutes

- 500g/1 lb cooked peeled prawns
- 1 garlic clove, crushed
- 2.5 cm/1 inch piece of fresh root ginger, peeled and diced
- 2 red chillies, chopped
- 1 bunch of coriander, chopped
- 2 teaspoons Thai fish sauce (*nam pla*)
- 1 egg yolk
- 250 g/8 oz mashed potatoes
- soy or chilli sauce, to serve

1 Place the prawns in a food processor or blender with the garlic, ginger, chillies, coriander, fish sauce and egg yolk. Process until smooth.

2 Remove the prawn mixture from the blender and mix it thoroughly with the mashed potatoes, using a fork. Divide the mixture into 12 cakes (or about 24 smaller ones), dusting your hands in flour if the mixture is sticky.

3 Heat the griddle pan. Place the prawn cakes on the griddle and cook for *5 minutes* on each side. Keep the batches warm while the remaining cakes are being cooked.

4 Serve with some soy or chilli sauce.

Serves 4

variation

Griddled Thai Fish Cakes

Preparation time: 15 minutes
Cooking time: 15 minutes

- 500 g/1 lb fillet of fish, cooked (such as salmon, cod or haddock)
- 1 garlic clove, crushed
- 2.5 cm/1 inch piece of fresh root ginger, peeled and diced
- 2 red chillies, chopped
- 1 bunch of coriander, chopped
- 250 g/8 oz mashed potatoes
- 1 egg yolk
- 2 teaspoons Thai fish sauce (*nam pla*)

1 Flake the fish, removing any bones, and place in a food processor or blender with the garlic, ginger, chillies, coriander, fish sauce and egg yolk. Process well until smooth.

2 Remove the fish mixture from the processor or blender and mix it thoroughly with the mashed potatoes, using a fork. Divide the mixture into 12 cakes (or about 24 smaller ones), dusting your hands in flour if the mixture is sticky.

3 Heat the griddle pan and complete the recipe following steps 3 and 4 of the main recipe.

Serves 4

Meat and Poultry

Griddling is a great way of cooking meat and poultry, relying as it does on the principle of searing food over heat to seal it on the outside and lock the flavour and juices inside. Use good-quality tender cuts of poultry, game and meat for the best results: they will look attractive and can be served with a variety of scrumptious sauces, salsas and chutneys and with griddled vegetables.

Devilled Chicken Breast

The tangy devil's sauce is also good with other griddled meats such as pork.

Preparation time: 15 minutes
Cooking time: 25–30 minutes

- 4 chicken breast fillets
- 4 raw beetroots, sliced

SAUCE:

- 2 tablespoons sunflower oil
- 1 onion, finely chopped
- 1 garlic clove, crushed
- 2 tablespoons white wine
- 4 tablespoons water
- 2 tablespoons brown sugar
- 1 tablespoon soy sauce
- 2 teaspoons Dijon mustard
- few drops of Tabasco
- 2 teaspoons chopped
  rosemary
- 2 teaspoons chopped
  parsley
- 1 teaspoon chopped thyme
- pepper

1 Heat the griddle and griddle the chicken for *8 minutes* each side, reduce heat, if necessary. Griddle the beetroot for *4–5 minutes* each side.

2 To make the sauce, heat the oil in a small saucepan, add the onion and garlic and cook for *2–3 minutes* until soft. Add the white wine, water, sugar, soy sauce, mustard, Tabasco and pepper to taste. Bring to the boil and simmer until the sauce is reduced by half and thick.

3 Just before serving, add the herbs to the sauce and serve with the griddled chicken fillets and beetroot.

Serves 4

Griddled Chicken with Peanut Sauce

This is a simple but delicious dish, which goes very well with a stir-fry of noodles and thin strips of vegetables tossed in sesame oil.

Preparation time: 5 minutes
Cooking time: 20 minutes

- 4 boneless chicken breasts
  or 8 boneless thighs
- 1 tablespoon soy sauce
- 2 tablespoons peanut butter,
  rough or smooth

- 4 tablespoons lemon juice
- 4 tablespoons water
- pepper

1 Heat the griddle pan. Cook the pieces of chicken for 6–8 *minutes* on each side or until the juices run clear when pierced with a knife.

2 Place the soy sauce, pepper to taste, peanut butter, lemon juice and water in a small saucepan, mix well and heat gently. Adjust the consistency with a little water if necessary.

3 When the chicken is cooked, serve with the peanut sauce drizzled over the top.

Serves 4

Griddled Tandoori Chicken

Preparation time: 10 minutes, plus marinating
Cooking time: 20 minutes

- 4 boneless chicken breasts
- 4 tablespoons tandoori paste
  or tandoori powder
- 2 onions, sliced
- 1 bunch of coriander,
  chopped

TO GARNISH:
- lemon wedges
- coriander sprigs

1 Remove the skin from the chicken, and make 3 slashes into the flesh of the chicken.

2 Rub the chicken with the tandoori paste or powder and leave to marinate, preferably overnight but *30 minutes* will do under rushed circumstances.

3 Heat the griddle pan. Place the breasts on the griddle and cook for *8–10 minutes* on each side, allowing a little charred colour to develop.

4 Add the sliced onions and griddle until slightly coloured. When the chicken and onions are cooked, mix the onions with the chopped coriander. Serve the chicken with the onion and coriander mixture and garnish with lemon wedges and coriander sprigs.

Serves 4

variation

Griddled Tandoori Lamb

Various cuts of lamb can be used for this, such as steaks from the leg or fillet from the loin. These are both quite expensive but cheaper cuts that can be used include the neck fillet or a boned shoulder of lamb. If you are using these cuts, marinate them first as in the main recipe, then cook them whole and carve them when cooked. They will take longer to cook because of their thickness and size.

Preparation time: 10 minutes
Cooking time: 20 minutes

- 4 x 175 g/6 oz pieces of lamb
  or 750 g/1½ lb piece of
  boneless lamb (see above)
- 4 tablespoons tandoori
  paste or tandoori powder
- 2 onions, sliced
- 1 bunch of coriander,
  chopped
- lemon wedges, to serve

1 Follow the instructions for the main recipe, replacing the chicken with the lamb. Pieces of lamb will need *6 minutes* on each side for pink meat and *8–10 minutes* on each side for well-done meat.

Serves 4

Griddled Duck with Oranges and Cranberries

Preparation time: 10 minutes
Cooking time: 20 minutes

- 4 Barbary duck breasts
- 2 oranges
- 125 g/4 oz cranberries
- 50 g/2 oz light brown sugar
- 1 tablespoon honey
- sea salt and pepper

1 Heat the griddle pan. Score the skin of the duck breast through to the flesh – this allows the fat to be released and the skin to go crispy.

2 Place the duck breasts on the griddle pan and cook them on the skin side for *6–10 minutes* and then on the other side for *4–6 minutes*.

3 Remove the rind and pith from the oranges. Then segment the oranges.

4 Place the prepared oranges, cranberries, sugar and seasoning in a saucepan and simmer to soften the cranberries. Finally, add the honey to the sauce.

5 Remove the duck from the griddle, slice and serve with the orange and cranberry sauce.

Serves 4

variation _____

Griddled Partridge with Orange and Cranberries

Preparation time: 15 minutes
Cooking time: 15 minutes

1 Follow the main recipe, replacing the duck with partridge breasts, but do not score the skin. Cook the partridge for *5–8 minutes* on each side.

Serves 4

Griddled Turkey with Citrus Chilli Sauce

Preparation time: 15 minutes
Cooking time: 25 minutes

- grated rind and juice of
  2 lemons
- 125 g/4 oz sugar
- 1 onion, finely chopped
- 2 chillies, finely chopped
- 1 garlic clove, crushed
- 3½ fl oz/100 ml water

- 4 x 175 g/6 oz turkey
  escalopes
- sea salt and pepper
- basmati rice, to serve
- basil leaves, torn, to garnish

1 Place the lemon rind and juice, sugar, onion, chillies, garlic and water in a small saucepan, and simmer gently for *15 minutes*. Watch this mixture carefully while it cooks, as it will burn easily.

2 Heat the griddle pan. Season the turkey escalopes well with salt and pepper and place on the griddle to cook for *5 minutes* on each side.

3 When the escalopes are cooked, serve on a bed of rice with the chilli sauce poured over and garnish with the torn basil leaves.

Serves 4

Fresh Fruit & Vegetables

Interesting fresh fruit and vegetables are available all year round and many are ideal for griddling – a quick and easy way of cooking fresh produce. Griddling brings out the natural flavour of fruit and vegetables; however, extra flavour can be easily added with the help of marinades, oils, and herbs, if liked.

Lemon

Vine Tomatoes

Lime

Peach

Baby courgette

Apricot

Baby aubergines

Cranberries

Lime is a citrus fruit with a tart flavour, which lends itself well to sweet and savoury dishes. Its tang is used to good effect in marinades.

Cranberries are small, tart, red berries, rich in vitamin C. They are ideal cooked and used in fruity sauces to serve with griddled poultry.

Lemon juice and rind are used to flavour a range of dishes including dressings and marinades. Lemon wedges may be griddled to serve as an attractive garnish.

Peach is a fruit which, because it has quite firm flesh, griddles well when sliced or halved. It looks good griddled

and is delicious served with crème fraîche or thick yogurt.

Vine tomatoes are tomatoes that have been ripened on the vine and are particularly tasty. They are rich in vitamins and are well suited to griddling.

Apricot is another fruit which, like the peach, griddles well when halved and stoned.

Baby courgettes have a sweet flavour and are very tender. They may be cut lengthways or into round slices for griddling.

Baby aubergines are sliced lengthways for griddling. They tend not to be as bitter as larger ones and therefore do not require salting before use.

Red onion

Baby leeks

Garlic

Plum tomatoes

Sweet Potato

Yellow pepper

Parsnip

Chestnut
Mushrooms

Red onion is characterized by its deep red skin. It is similar to the Spanish onion in size, but milder and sweeter. It may be cut into wedges with the roots left intact or sliced into rings for griddling.

Chestnut mushrooms are a variety of cultivated mushroom with a brown cap and a strong flavour. Simply wipe them before use – they do not need peeling.

Baby leeks benefit from simple cooking, which brings out their delicate flavour. They taste wonderful simply griddled and tossed in balsamic vinegar.

Sweet potato has a distinctive sweet, chestnutty flavour. Despite its name it is no relation to the potato, but can be cooked in the same way.

Parsnip has an unusual sweet flavour which, when griddled, goes particularly well with griddled beetroot.

Garlic is the most pungent of the onion family. The cloves are best griddled whole, either peeled or in their skins.

Plum tomatoes are richly flavoured with dense flesh and small seed clusters.

Yellow pepper is sweet in flavour and rich in vitamin C. It is ideal for griddling or tossing in a salad to accompany griddled meat or poultry.

Griddled Veal Chops with Gremolata

This is a tasty but simple way to serve veal chops. Gremolata is classically served with *osso bucco* but it goes well with almost any simply cooked meat.

Preparation time: 10 minutes
Cooking time: 12 minutes

- 4 veal chops
- 1 bunch of oregano, chopped
- grated rind of 2 lemons
- 2 garlic cloves, crushed
- 1 bunch of parsley, finely chopped
- sea salt and pepper
- fresh pasta, to serve

1 Heat the griddle pan. Rub the veal chops with the chopped oregano and seasoning, place on the griddle and cook for *6 minutes* on each side, depending on thickness.

2 To make the gremolata, mix together the lemon rind, garlic and parsley, and season with salt and pepper.

3 Serve the veal chops with fresh pasta and a good spoonful of gremolata on top of the chops as well as a drizzle of olive oil, if liked.

Serves 4

Griddled Lamb in Naan Bread with Fresh Mint Salad

Preparation time: 20 minutes
Cooking time: 12 minutes

- **750 g/1½ lb minced lamb**
- **1 bunch of parsley, chopped**
- **1 onion, chopped**
- **1 garlic clove, crushed**
- **a dash of Tabasco**
- **1 egg, beaten**
- **4 small naan breads**
- **1 red onion, sliced**
- **3 tomatoes, halved and finely sliced**
- **1 large bunch of mint, chopped**
- **2 tablespoons olive oil**
- **2 tablespoons lemon juice**
- **sea salt and pepper**

1 Mix together the lamb, parsley, onion, garlic, Tabasco, egg, salt and pepper. Shape into 8 sausages that will fit into the naan breads.

2 Heat the griddle pan. Place the lamb sausages on the griddle and cook for *6–9 minutes*. Take care when turning the sausages – it is important to get a good crust on the outside of the sausages so that they don't break when turned.

3 Mix together the onion, tomatoes, mint, olive oil, lemon juice and seasoning. Open the naan breads carefully, making a pocket in which to place the filling.

4 Place the naan breads under a medium grill and cook on each side until lightly browned. Fill with the salad and add the lamb sausages. Serve immediately.

Serves 4

variation _____

Griddled Pork in Naan Bread with Mint

Preparation time: 20 minutes
Cooking time: 15 minutes

1 Follow the instructions for the main recipe, using minced pork instead of lamb. Cook the pork sausages for *9 minutes*.

Serves 4

Griddled Gammon with Apricot Salsa

This is a simple yet effective recipe, and the apricot salsa is the perfect accompaniment for the gammon. If fresh apricots are unavailable, you can use either dried apricots that have been soaked, or the kind that require no soaking.

Preparation time: 20 minutes
Cooking time: 25–35 minutes

- 4 x 175 g/6 oz gammon
  steaks

APRICOT SALSA:

- 250 g/8 oz fresh apricots,
  pitted and chopped
- grated rind and juice of
  1 lime

- 2 teaspoons fresh root
  ginger, finely diced
- 2 teaspoons clear honey
- 1 tablespoon olive oil
- 2 tablespoons chopped sage
- 4 spring onions, chopped
- sea salt and pepper

1 Heat the griddle pan. Put on the gammon steaks in batches and cook for *4 minutes* on each side. Keep warm until they are all cooked.

2 To make the salsa, mix together the apricots, lime rind and juice, ginger, honey, olive oil and sage in a small bowl. Crush the mixture with the back of a fork. Add the spring onions and season, mixing well. Serve the gammon steaks immediately, topped with the apricot salsa.

Serves 4

Griddled Italian Lamb with Rosemary Oil

Use loin fillets, which are expensive, or the much cheaper neck fillets.

Preparation time: 20 minutes
Cooking time: 20–40 minutes

- 2 lamb fillets, trimmed of fat, weighing about 750 g/1½ lb
- 4 garlic cloves, cut into slivers
- a few small sprigs of rosemary
- 2 red onions, quartered
- 1 tablespoon chopped rosemary
- 4 tablespoons olive oil
- sea salt and pepper

TO SERVE:
- fresh pasta
- Parmesan cheese shavings

1 Make small incisions with a sharp knife all over the fillets and insert the garlic slivers and rosemary sprigs. Heat the griddle pan, put on the fillets, and cook, turning the lamb occasionally, until charred all over, about *20 minutes* for rare, or *30–40 minutes* for well done. Add the onions for the last *10 minutes* and char on the outside.

2 Place the chopped rosemary and oil in a mortar and crush with a pestle to release the flavours. Season. Allow the lamb to rest for *5 minutes* before carving into slices. Spoon the rosemary oil over the top and serve at once with the griddled onions. Serve with fresh pasta, lightly tossed in olive oil, and Parmesan shavings.

Serves 4

Pork Escalopes Griddled with Peach Chutney

This peach chutney is a lovely accompaniment to meat. Use fresh peaches when they are in season, otherwise use dried, and soak them for a couple of hours. If you like food hot and spicy, a sprinkling of dried chillies can be added to the chutney.

Preparation time: 10 minutes
Cooking time: 20 minutes

- **4 x 175 g/6 oz pork escalopes, sliced**

PEACH CHUTNEY:
- **4 fresh peaches**
- **1 tablespoon olive oil**
- **1 onion, sliced**
- **1 tablespoon vinegar**
- **2 tablespoons brown sugar**
- **2 teaspoons mustard seeds**
- **sea salt and pepper**
- **sprigs of oregano, to garnish**

1 Start by making the peach chutney. Bring a saucepan of water to the boil and make a cross in the skin of the peaches. Plunge the peaches into the boiling water for *10 seconds*. Remove and peel away the skin. Cut the peach flesh away from the stone and into wedges.

2 Gently heat the oil in a saucepan, add the sliced onion and cook until soft. Add the peach to the onion along with the vinegar, sugar and mustard seeds, season to taste with salt and pepper. Allow to simmer gently for *10 minutes*, watching that it does not stick on the bottom of the pan. Add a little water if it looks like drying out.

3 Heat the griddle pan. Cook the escalopes for *4–5 minutes* on each side depending on their thickness, or until cooked.

4 Serve the escalopes with the chutney and garnished with sprigs of oregano. A good accompaniment is some roasted root vegetables, such as beetroot, parsnips, turnips, carrots and potatoes.

Serves 4

variation ———————————————

Chicken Escalopes Griddled with Peach Chutney

Preparation time: 10 minutes
Cooking time: 20 minutes

- **4 small chicken breasts, flattened between clingfilm with a rolling pin and sliced**
- **Peach Chutney (see main recipe), to serve**

1 Heat the griddle pan. Cook the slices of chicken for *3–4 minutes* on each side or until cooked.

2 Serve the chicken with the peach chutney and a selection of griddled or lightly steamed vegetables.

Serves 4

Pork Fillet with Griddled Onions and Apples

Preparation time: 20 minutes
Cooking time: 40 minutes

- 750 g/1½ lb fillet of pork, trimmed
- 4 garlic cloves, sliced lengthways
- 1 large sprig of rosemary, broken into small lengths
- 2 red onions, cut into wedges, root left intact
- 2 dessert apples
- sea salt and pepper

1 Make small incisions with a sharp knife evenly over the whole length of the pork fillet and then insert the garlic and pieces of rosemary into the pork, making sure that they are firmly in place. Season to taste with salt and pepper.

2 Heat the griddle pan. Place the pork on the griddle and cook on a moderate heat for *30 minutes*, turning the meat to get an evenly griddled crust. Add the red onions and cook for *3 minutes* on each side.

3 Remove the pork from the griddle and allow to rest for *5 minutes*.

4 Cut the apple into wedges and core. Put the apple wedges on the griddle pan and cook on each side for *2–3 minutes*.

5 Carve the pork fillet into 2.5 cm/1 inch slices and serve with the onion and apple wedges.

Serves 4

Mixed Pepper-Crusted Venison Fillet

Preparation time: 10 minutes
Cooking time: up to 45 minutes
Oven temperature: 200°C (400°F), Gas Mark 6

- **750g/1½ lb fillet of venison, cut from the haunch**
- **75 g/3 oz mixed peppercorns, crushed**
- **25 g/1 oz juniper berries, crushed**
- **1 egg white**
- **sea salt**

TO SERVE:
- **redcurrant jelly**
- **pink sweet potato chips**

1 Make sure that the venison fits into the griddle pan, and cut the fillet in half, if necessary, to fit. Heat the griddle pan to a hot temperature.

2 Mix the peppercorns, juniper berries and salt together and place on a large shallow dish. Dip the venison into the egg white, then roll the venison in the peppercorn mix, covering all over with an even layer of the crust ingredients.

3 Cook the venison on the griddle for *4 minutes* on each side, turning carefully so that the crust stays intact. Cook evenly on all sides, then transfer the fillet to a lightly oiled roasting tin and cook in a preheated oven, 200°C (400°F), Gas Mark 6, for a further *15 minutes* for rare, and up to *30 minutes* for well done. This depends on the thickness of the venison fillet.

4 Serve the venison with redcurrant jelly and finely sliced, pink sweet potato chips.

Serves 4

Griddled Sausages with Mustard Mash

Preparation time: 10 minutes
Cooking time: 25 minutes

- 8 speciality sausages
- 2 onions, cut into wedges, roots left intact

MUSTARD MASH:
- 1 kg/2 lb potatoes, quartered but left unpeeled
- 75 g/3 oz butter
- 1 tablespoon wholegrain mustard

- 3 teaspoons English mustard
- 1 garlic clove, crushed
- 1 large bunch of parsley, chopped
- a dash of olive oil
- sea salt and pepper

1 Heat the griddle pan.

2 Place the potatoes in a saucepan of cold water, bring to the boil and simmer for *15 minutes.*

3 Place the sausages on the griddle and cook for *10 minutes*, turning to get an even colour. Add the onion wedges and cook for *6–7 minutes* with the sausages.

4 When the potatoes are cooked, drain well and return to the pan, place over a low heat and allow any excess water to steam away, without colouring the potatoes. Remove from the heat and peel. Then mash them well, add the butter, mustards and garlic and salt and pepper, and continue to mash. Taste the potato and add more mustard if liked. Finally, add the parsley and a dash of olive oil and stir.

5 Serve the mash and sausages together with the griddled onion wedges.

Serves 4

variation _____

Griddled Liver with Mustard Mash

Preparation time: 10 minutes
Cooking time: 25 minutes

- 750 g/1½ lb calf or lambs' liver, finely sliced
- balsamic vinegar, to drizzle

- sea salt and pepper
- Mustard Mash (see main recipe), to serve

1 Cook the slices of liver quickly on a very hot griddle for *1½–2 minutes* on each side until it is cooked but still pink in the middle.

2 Add a little balsamic vinegar to the pan and heat up and pour over the liver. Season the cooked liver to taste with salt and pepper and serve with the mustard mash.

Serves 4

Desserts

For dessert lovers griddling fruit is an exciting and very quick way of producing the finale to a meal. Griddled fresh fruit looks appetizing and is delicious served with simple sauces such as chocolate or caramel, and with clotted cream, or crème fraîche for a healthier option. Griddled cakes are tasty, too, served with ice cream and drizzled with maple syrup.

Griddled Pears with Chocolate Sauce

Preparation time: 10 minutes
Cooking time: 10 minutes

- **4 pears**
- **50 g/2 oz flaked almonds, toasted**

CHOCOLATE SAUCE:
- **175 g/6 oz good-quality dark chocolate**
- **3 tablespoons water**
- **1 tablespoon golden syrup**
- **15 g/½ oz butter**

1 To make the chocolate sauce, first make a bain-marie. Half fill a small saucepan with water, then fit an ovenproof bowl into the saucepan so that the bottom of the bowl is just immersed in the water. Place the bain-marie on the heat and allow the water to simmer gently. Add the chocolate, water, golden syrup and butter, allow to melt and mix together until the chocolate sauce is glossy and smooth.

2 Heat the griddle pan.

3 Peel the pears, if wished, cut into quarters and core. Place on the griddle pan to cook for *2–3 minutes* on each side.

4 Serve the griddled pears with the chocolate sauce drizzled over, and sprinkled with flaked almonds. To make this a really wicked pudding serve with a spoon of clotted cream or a scoop of ice cream.

Serves 4

Griddled Bananas with Chocolate and Honey

These delicious bananas can also be cooked on a barbecue, an ideal dessert for warm summer evenings.

Preparation time: 5 minutes
Cooking time: 10 minutes

- 4 ripe bananas
- 75 g/3 oz good-quality dark chocolate
- 75 g/3 oz white chocolate
- 4 tablespoons runny honey

1 Heat the griddle pan. Place the bananas, still in their skins, on the griddle and cook for about *10 minutes*, turning constantly, by which time the skins will have gone black.

2 Grate the dark and white chocolate and mix the two together.

3 When the bananas are cooked, peel them and cut in half lengthways. Drizzle the honey along the length, and then sprinkle with the grated chocolate.

Serves 4

Panettone with Griddled Apples and Clotted Cream

This is so simple to make and yet a joy to eat. Experiment with various apples – Bramleys work well as they are so sharp but eating apples also work well.

Preparation time: 10 minutes
Cooking time: 10 minutes

- 75 g/3 oz brown sugar
- 3 tablespoons water
- 75 g/3 oz butter
- 4 apples, cored and cut into wedges

- 4 slices of panettone
- 75 g/3 oz clotted cream
- ground cinnamon, to dust

1 Heat the griddle pan. Place the sugar, water and butter in a small saucepan and simmer to make a smooth caramel sauce. Remove from the heat.

2 Place the apples on the griddle and cook on each side for *2–3 minutes*.

3 Place the slices of panettone on the griddle and cook on each side until toasted.

4 Place the panettone on 4 plates and top with the apple wedges. Spoon over the caramel sauce, add a spoon of clotted cream and lightly dust with ground cinnamon.

Serves 4

Sweet Bruschetta with Plums and Cinnamon

Preparation time: 10 minutes
Cooking time: 10 minutes

- 75 g/3 oz brown sugar
- 3 tablespoons water
- 75 g/3 oz butter
- 8 plums, more if they are small

- 4 slices of bread
- 150 g/5 oz Greek yogurt
- ground cinnamon, to dust

1 Place the sugar, water and butter in a small saucepan and simmer to make a smooth caramel sauce. Remove from the heat and set aside.

2 Heat the griddle pan. Cut the plums in half and remove the stones if they are large or leave whole if small. Place them on the griddle and cook for *5 minutes*, turning constantly.

3 Place the bread either on the griddle to toast or in a toaster.

4 Arrange the toast on 4 plates, add the griddled plums and Greek yogurt. Spoon over the caramel sauce and dust the plums with cinnamon.

Serves 4

Griddled Cakes with Ice Cream and Maple Syrup

Preparation time: 10 minutes
Cooking time: 10 minutes

- **1 large egg**
- **3 dessertspoons vegetable oil**
- **75 g/3 oz self-raising flour**
- **15 g/½ oz sugar**
- **150 ml/¼ pint milk**
- **8 scoops of ice cream**
- **bottled maple syrup, to serve**

1 To make the cake batter, place the egg, oil, flour, sugar and milk in a food processor or blender and process until a smooth creamy consistency is reached.

2 Heat the griddle pan to a medium heat and place one-third of the batter in separate corners of the griddle, making 4 separate cakes.

3 After about *1 minute*, the bottoms of the cakes will form a crust, the tops will start to set and air bubbles will rise. Using a fish slice, carefully turn over and cook on the other side for *1 minute*.

4 Repeat twice more until all the batter is used – making 12 cakes in all. Serve 3 cakes per person, with scoops of ice cream and maple sauce drizzled over the top.

Serves 4

Apricots and Nectarines Griddled with Honey and Yogurt

This is a simple pudding, but in the midst of the summer season when these fruits are abundantly available, it makes a quick and tasty pudding that looks and tastes luxuriously rich and delicious.

Preparation time: 5 minutes
Cooking time: 6 minutes

- 4 nectarines, halved and stoned
- 8 apricots, halved and stoned
- 150 g/5 oz Greek yogurt
- 4 dessertspoons Greek runny honey

1 Heat the griddle pan.

2 Place the nectarines and apricots on the griddle and cook for *2–3 minutes* on each side.

3 Serve the fruit arranged on plates with spoonfuls of Greek yogurt and drizzled with Greek honey. The fruit can be served hot or at room temperature.

Serves 4

Pineapple with Hazelnuts and Crème Fraîche

Pineapple works so well on the griddle because of its high natural sugar content which gives really dramatic griddle pan lines.

Preparation time: 5 minutes
Cooking time: 5 minutes

- 1 pineapple, peeled, halved lengthways and sliced
- 125 g/4 oz roasted hazelnuts, chopped
- 125 g/4 oz crème fraîche

1 Heat the griddle pan.

2 Place the pineapple slices on the griddle pan and cook for *1–2 minutes* on each side.

3 Mix the hazelnuts into the crème fraîche.

4 Serve the griddled pineapple with the nutty crème fraîche spooned over it.

Serves 4

Special Photography:
Philip Webb
Jacket Photography:
Philip Webb
Other Photography:
Reed Consumer Books Ltd./
Jean Cazals, Sandra Lane
Home Economist:
Fran Warde